# DISCOVERING NATIVE NORTH AMERICAN CULTURES

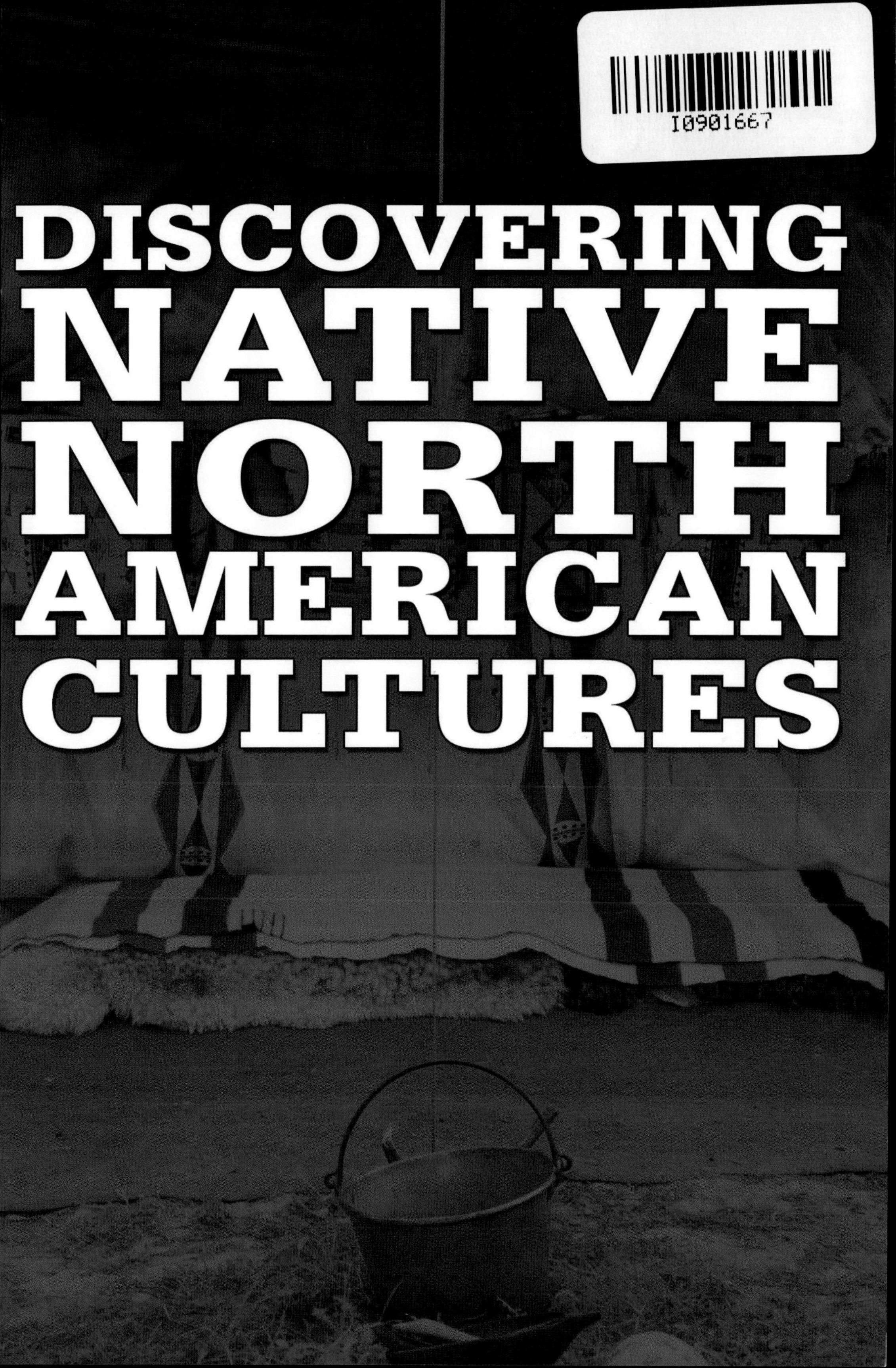

EXPLORING ANCIENT CIVILIZATIONS

# DISCOVERING NATIVE NORTH AMERICAN CULTURES

JUSTINE CIOVACCO

Britannica
Educational Publishing
IN ASSOCIATION WITH
ROSEN
EDUCATIONAL SERVICES

Published in 2015 by Britannica Educational Publishing (a trademark of Encyclopædia Britannica, Inc.)
in association with The Rosen Publishing Group, Inc.
29 East 21st Street, New York, NY 10010



Distributed exclusively by Rosen Publishing.
To see additional Britannica Educational Publishing titles, go to rosenpublishing.com.

First Edition

**Britannica Educational Publishing**
J. E. Luebering: Director, Core Reference Group
Anthony L. Green: Editor, Compton's by Britannica

**Rosen Publishing**
Hope Lourie Killcoyne: Executive Editor
Tracey Baptiste: Editor
Nelson Sá: Art Director
Michael Moy: Designer
Cindy Reiman: Photography Manager

**Library of Congress Cataloging-in-Publication Data**

Ciovacco, Justine.
Discovering native North American cultures/Justine Ciovacco.—First edition
pages cm.—(Exploring ancient civilizations)
Includes bibliographical references and index.
ISBN 978-1-62275-825-8 (library bound) — ISBN 978-1-62275-824-1 (pbk.) —
ISBN 978-1-62275-823-4 (6-pack)
1. Indians of North America—Juvenile literature. I. Title.
E77.4.C568 2015
970.004'97—dc23

2014024430

*Manufactured in the United States of America.*

**Photo Credits:**
Cover, pp. 1, 3 © iStockphoto.com/aguirre mar; p. 7 Doug James/Shutterstock.com; pp. 9, 12, 13 Encyclopædia Britannica, Inc.; pp. 11, 40 © AP Images; p. 16 Library of Congress Prints and Photographs Division; p. 17 Private Collection/Peter Newark American Pictures/Bridgeman Images; p. 18 Library of Congress, Washington, D.C. (neg. no. LC-USZ62-51063); pp. 20, 26 Universal Images Group/Getty Images; p. 21 Wayne R Bilenduke/The Image Bank/Getty Images; p. 25 Private Collection/The Stapleton Collection/Bridgeman Images; p. 29 The Bridgeman Art Library/Getty Images; p. 31 Buyenlarge/Archive Photos/Getty Images; p. 33 Stephen Shugerman/Getty Images; p. 35 Hyoung Chang/Denver Post/Getty Images; p. 38 Tim Graham/Hulton Archive/Getty Images; p. 41 David Edwards/National Geographic Image Collection/Getty Images; p. 42 Rebecca Cook/Reuters/Landov; cover and interior graphics © iStockphoto.com/professorphotoshop; (patterned banners and borders), HorenkO/Shutterstock.com and Freckles/Shutterstock.com (background textures).

# CONTENTS

# INTRODUCTION

The first people in North America lived there thousands of years before European explorers arrived. These people had trekked into North America from Siberia, a large area that is now part of Russia. They began to cross a land bridge into North America more than thirteen thousand years ago, when the Ice Age was coming to an end.

No one knows how many native people first settled in Northern America (present-day United States and Canada). Population estimates for the time of Christopher Columbus's arrival in 1492 are of nine hundred thousand to eighteen million living north of the Rio Grande. Many descendants of these native people still live in North America today. Arctic peoples, including the Eskimo and the Aleut, still live in the far northern parts of North America.

Life changed greatly for North America's natives with the arrival of Europeans in their lands, the passage of time, and the modernization of society.

A dancer participates in the annual Red Mountain Eagle Pow-Wow in Scottsdale, Arizona.

## CHAPTER ONE

# THE FIRST PEOPLES OF THE AMERICAS

The first people in North America arrived during the last Ice Age, when thick ice sheets covered much of the northern part of the continent. As the ice sheets absorbed water, sea levels dropped and a land bridge emerged along the present-day Bering Strait. From about thirty thousand to twelve thousand years ago the land bridge connected northeastern Asia to what is now Alaska. Humans began to cross over from Asia at least thirteen thousand years ago. When the ice sheets melted, the land bridge disappeared under the rising seas and the migration ended.

## Into the Americas

These people traveled southward through North America. Some followed the Pacific coast, perhaps combining walking with boat travel. Others found ice-free routes east of the Rocky Mountains that led into the heart of the continent.

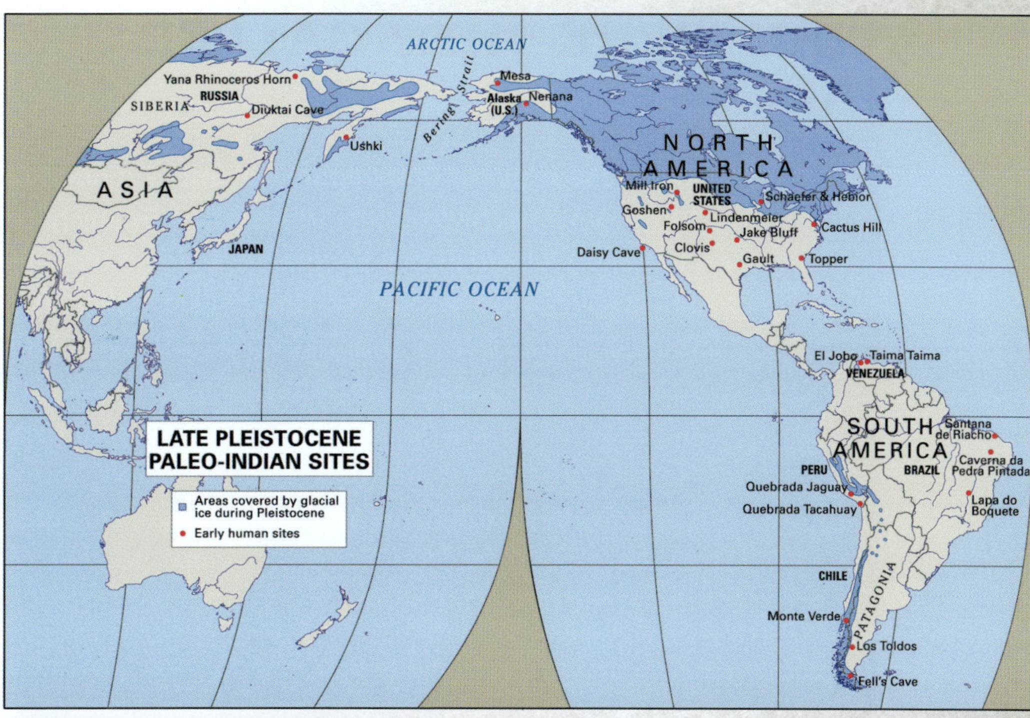


**The locations of archaeological sites in the Americas suggest the migration routes followed by Paleo-Indians after the glaciers of the late Pleistocene Epoch melted.**

As the ice continued to melt over time, the land gradually opened up. This enabled people to spread out across North America and down through Central America into South America. Historians believe one group after another continued to move farther down through the continent over many centuries.

## WHY WERE THEY CALLED INDIANS?

When the explorer Christopher Columbus landed in the New World, he used the term *Indios* (Spanish for "Indians") for the native people because he thought he had reached a part of South Asia called the Indies. In the 1960s many activists in the United States and Canada rejected the label "Indians" because of its mistaken origin. In these countries Native Americans became the preferred term. Later, Native Americans in Canada began to refer to themselves as First Nations. Various peoples of the Arctic prefer the terms "Alaska Native," "Yupik," or "Inuit." Canadians of mixed First Nations and European heritage are known as Métis. Yet even with this great variety of terms, many native people of North America continue to identify themselves as Indians.

## Paleo-Indians

The earliest people of North America are called Paleo-Indians. The prefix "paleo" comes from a Greek word meaning "early" or "ancient." The Paleo-Indians shared some cultural traits with peoples of Asia, such as the use of fire and domesticated

**Paleo-Indians used tools such as this Goshen projectile point to hunt huge game animals.**

dogs. However, they do not seem to have used other Old World technologies, such as grazing animals, domesticated plants, and the wheel.

The Paleo-Indians were hunters and gatherers. They lived in small, family-based groups called bands that moved from place to place in search of food. They shared the land with large mammals such as mammoths, mastodons, and giant bison. Archaeological sites of Paleo-Indians often include bones from these animals. This has sometimes led to the mistaken idea that

**Mastodons and wolly mammoths were hunted by some Paleo-Indians. These animals were similar in size to modern African elephants but, unlike the modern variety, they were adapted to Ice Age temperatures.**

these people only hunted and ate large animals. By the turn of the twenty-first century, however, digs by archaeologists showed that Paleo-Indians ate both animals and wild plants, including fruit, tubers, and seaweed. Evidence also has shown that some Paleo-Indians fished.

## Archaic Cultures

The Archaic cultures developed from Paleo-Indian traditions. They arose in

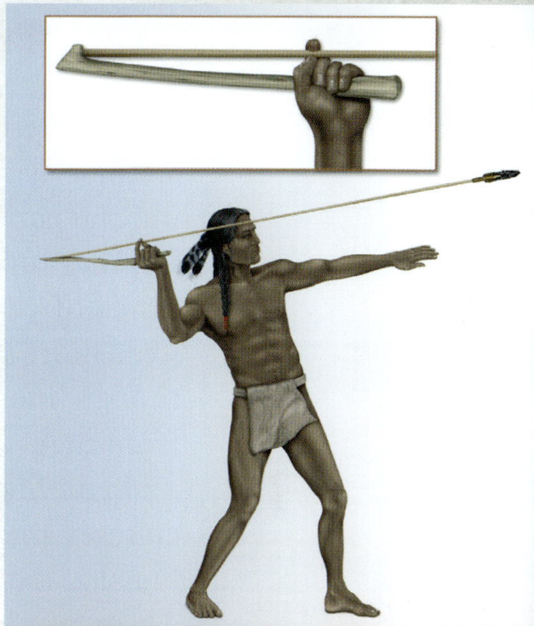

The spear-thrower was an innovation of the Archaic period. It consisted of a rod with a hook at the rear end to hold the weapon in place until its release. The device gave greater velocity and force to the spear.

response to environmental changes. Beginning about 11,500 years ago, temperatures rose dramatically worldwide. Very large animals such as mammoths could not cope with the change and became extinct. Other animals, such as bison, survived by becoming smaller. At the same time new grasses, trees, and other plants developed.

As the environment changed, so did the Indians' lifestyles. The most visible change was in their diet. Archaic peoples used a wider range of plant and animal foods than the Paleo-Indians had. They relied more upon smaller animals such as deer and elk. They caught more fish and collected more shellfish from rivers and lakes. They also gathered seeds, an addition to the larger plant foods of the Paleo-Indians, such as fruit and roots. In the late Archaic period, people began to farm. The Archaic period lasted until about 2000 BCE in most of North America.

## Prehistoric Farmers

In Northern America the change from an Archaic way of life based mainly on hunting and gathering to one more dependent on farming took from a few hundred to thousands of years. Prehistoric farming peoples lived more settled lives than Archaic groups, though most still did some hunting away from their villages.

In the first centuries CE three major farming cultures arose in the Southwest: the Ancestral Pueblo, the Mogollon, and the Hohokam. These peoples developed irrigation systems to bring water to their fields of corn, squash, and beans. The Ancestral Pueblo are also famous for their cliff dwellings. These apartment-style buildings had as many as one thousand rooms and up to four stories.

East of the Mississippi River, the best-known prehistoric faming culture was the Mississippian. It was based on the production of corn. Mississippian people lived in large towns governed by priest-rulers. The largest town was at Cahokia, near present-day Saint Louis, MO. At its peak, it housed ten thousand to twenty thousand people.

## CHAPTER TWO

# NATIVE PEOPLES SPREAD TO DIFFERENT PARTS OF NORTH AMERICA

As the native people of North America spread out across the continent, they formed hundreds of groups that are usually called nations or tribes. Today there are more than 560 federally recognized tribes in the United States alone. However, it is hard to know how many groups existed in prehistoric times. Neighboring tribes often had similar ways of life. For this reason, historians have grouped tribes into culture areas. These are geographic regions in which the people shared certain traits. For example, they often had similar ways of farming, hunting, and finding shelter. Although tribes had their own languages, the languages spoken within a culture area were typically related to one another.

Me-Na-Wa, a chief of the Creek people.

## Native Peoples of Eastern North America

Native Americans in eastern North America included the Iroquois in the Northeast and the Cherokee and Creek in the Southeast. People in these regions used tree bark and branches to make houses, weapons, tools, and canoes. They made clothing from the skins of deer and other animals. They hunted, fished, and gathered wild plants. They also planted corn, squash, beans, and tobacco.

An Iroquois chief is shown wearing an animal pelt.

## Native Peoples of the Great Plains

Native peoples living on the Great Plains of central North America included the Cheyenne and the Sioux. The grasses of the plains fed huge herds of grazing animals, including elk, deer, antelope, and bison. Plains Indians got almost everything they needed from the bison. They ate the meat, made tepees (cone-shaped homes) and clothing from the skins, and created tools from the bones.

**A Paiute family of the early twentieth century rests outside their wickiup.**

## Native Peoples of Western North America

A large number of nations lived along the Pacific coast. Those who settled in what is now California fished and hunted, and many groups made flour from acorns. Dome- and cone-shaped houses were the most typical types in this area, though some groups, such as the Miwok, built houses that were partly underground.

The Tlingit and the Kwakiutl are among the nations that lived on the Northwest coast, an area that stretches between modern California and Alaska. The people of this region fished in the ocean and rivers. Some groups hunted whales. They made large houses and sturdy canoes out of wood.

The peoples of the dry Southwest included the Pueblo, the Navajo, and the Apache. Some Southwest Indians relied almost entirely on farming for food. They used irrigation to water their fields. Other peoples relied more on hunting and gathering. The most remarkable dwellings in the Southwest were the apartment houses built by the Pueblo. They were made from stone and adobe.

The Great Basin was home to the Shoshone, the Paiute, and other peoples. Great Basin peoples were nomadic, traveling through the desert in search of food. They hunted small animals, fished, and gathered berries, nuts, seeds, and roots.

North of this region lived the Nez Percé, the Flathead, and other groups of Plateau Indians. People in these nations fished, hunted, and gathered roots and bulbs to eat. They lived in villages during winter. During summer they camped in good hunting and gathering spots.

# PRESERVING FOOD

The climate of the Subarctic is cool, and the landscape is harsh, so it was not always easy to find food. Native people had to find ways to save food for times when it could not be found. Subarctic peoples preserved meat by drying and pounding it together with melted fat and dried berries to make a food called pemmican. Near the Pacific, the Indians preserved salmon by smoking it.

This drawing depicts an Inuit-Yupik family.

## Native Peoples of the Arctic and Subarctic

The northernmost lands of North America make up the Arctic culture area. This region lies near and above the Arctic Circle and includes parts of present-day Alaska and Canada. South of that is an area called the Subarctic.

**An Inuit family sits inside an igloo in Canada.**

Temperatures in the Arctic are very cold for most of the year, and winters are especially harsh. Native peoples were traditionally hunters and gatherers. Some nations moved with the seasons in search of food. The native peoples of the Arctic include the Inuit, Inupiat, Yupik, and Alutiit. These groups are more closely related to people in Asia than to the groups to their south

## SOCIAL GROUPS

Most native people lived in small communities that worked together to make important decisions. The most important social group for most native peoples was the nuclear or extended family. The clan was a larger family group. Members of a clan might live in different villages, but they claimed descent from a common ancestor. Men and women were required to marry outside their clan. Groups of native families joined to form bands. The families in a band lived, worked, and traveled together. Membership was generally based on a combination of kinship, marriage, and friendship. The next level of social organization was the tribe or nation, which was made up of a number of bands or neighboring villages. Tribal members were usually linked by ties of kinship, language, and cultural traditions.

in the modern United States and Canada. Therefore, scholars generally separate the Arctic people from natives who lived farther south. This is why many Alaskan groups prefer to be called Alaska Natives rather than Native Americans. Most of Canada's Arctic people prefer the name Inuit.

The Chipewyan and the Cree were among the nations living in the Subarctic. In this area, the climate is cool but not as cold as the Arctic. The land is fairly flat and covered mostly by swampy evergreen forest. Subarctic nations depended on caribou, moose, and beavers for food. They also made tepees and clothing from animal hides.

## CHAPTER THREE

# EUROPEANS ARRIVE IN NORTH AMERICA

Native people had lived in the Americas for thousands of years before the first European explorers arrived. Early explorers and settlers tended to think of the native people—or Indians, as they called them—as a single group of people, but the native peoples themselves did not. Each considered himself or herself to be a member of one of the hundreds of nations in the Americas. The name of many nations meant "the people" in those nations' languages.

## Europeans and Native North Americans

By the time Europeans encountered native peoples, there was amazing cultural diversity in Northern America. Native groups had more than fifty language families with between three hundred and five hundred languages, as well as different types of food, clothing, and shelter.

**The Vikings are believed to be the first Europeans who arrived in the Americas.**

Viking explorer Leif Eriksson landed in North America around 1000. Conflicts with the native peoples soon forced the Vikings out. In 1492, Italian explorer Christopher Columbus had more luck. He was searching for a sea route from Europe to Asia, but his trip—sponsored by King Ferdinand and Queen Isabella of Spain—brought new lands and resources to light. The Europeans called it the New World. Spain went on to conquer the Aztec in Mexico and the Inca in South America before colonizing the Southeast, the Southwest, and California.

Other European countries also looked for opportunities in the New World. France focused mainly on trade and shipping. It claimed parts of the Northeast, the Southeast, and the Subarctic. England's leaders were eager for land. In the early 1600s, the English began establishing colonies along the Atlantic coast from New England to Virginia. Later, in the 1700s, Russia occupied the northern Pacific coast to collect sea otter furs for trade with China.

Some Native Americans helped the English at first. However, as more English colonists arrived, they took over more land. Several wars broke out between colonists and native people. An early clash called the Pequot War took place in Connecticut in 1636, when colonists attacked the main village of the Pequot. About six hundred Native Americans were killed, and the Pequot nation was virtually destroyed. In 1675, various Native American nations in New England formed an alliance to work against European settlement. It was led by Metacom, who was called King Philip by the colonists. In the ensuing King

**The Battle of Bloody Brook (September 18, 1675) was one of the conflicts during King Philip's War.**

Philip's War (1675–1676) about six hundred Europeans and three thousand Native Americans from several nations were killed. This European victory allowed colonists to settle more land in New England.

## The Effects of Colonization

The arrival of Europeans in the Americas proved to be devastating. Military battles and European diseases, including measles

## WHO WAS KING PHILIP?

Metacom (*c.* 1638–1676), also called Metacomet, was a Native American leader of the Wampanoag nation. He was the second son of Massasoit, a grand chief of the Wampanoag who oversaw peaceful relations with colonists. After his father died and his brother Wamsutta became chief, Metacom and his brother requested English names from the colonial court of the Plymouth settlement. Metacom received the name Philip, and Wamsutta was called Alexander. Philip became chief when Alexander died.

## EUROPEANS BRING NEW WEAPONS OF WAR

**In the eastern Great Lakes region, the Iroquois and the Huron competed to get a greater share of the fur trade with Europeans. The Huron joined forces with the French, who gave them iron axes to defeat the Iroquois. After 1620, however, the Iroquois fought back with guns given to them by their allies, the Dutch and the English. The new weaponry forever changed warfare among native peoples.**

and smallpox, killed millions of native people. Many survivors lost their land and were forced into slavery by the Europeans. Native peoples were also subject to discriminatory political and legal policies, as they were put under the rule of colonial authorities and, later, federal and state governments. This history of injustice largely explains why native peoples are among the poorest groups in the United States and Canada.

Despite many hardships, there were some favorable changes with the Europeans' arrival. The Europeans brought new plants and animals to their "New World." The

**A group of Cheyenne travels on horseback.**

horse, in particular, brought great change. Groups on horseback could travel long distances, plow land, and hunt bison much more easily than before. Native peoples also welcomed such European goods as cloth fabrics and metal tools.

## CHAPTER FOUR

# NATIVE AMERICANS' RELATIONSHIPS WITH THE UNITED STATES AND CANADA

Colonists had taken over much of the land in the Northeast by the end of the American Revolution in 1783. The new U.S. government hoped to maintain peace with Native Americans, promising that native land rights would be honored. Nevertheless, settlers continued to move westward, building and farming on native lands. This brought decades of conflict.

## Treaties and Battles

By the 1830s, the U.S. government focused on moving Native Americans to areas west of the Mississippi River—specifically, the Great Plains.

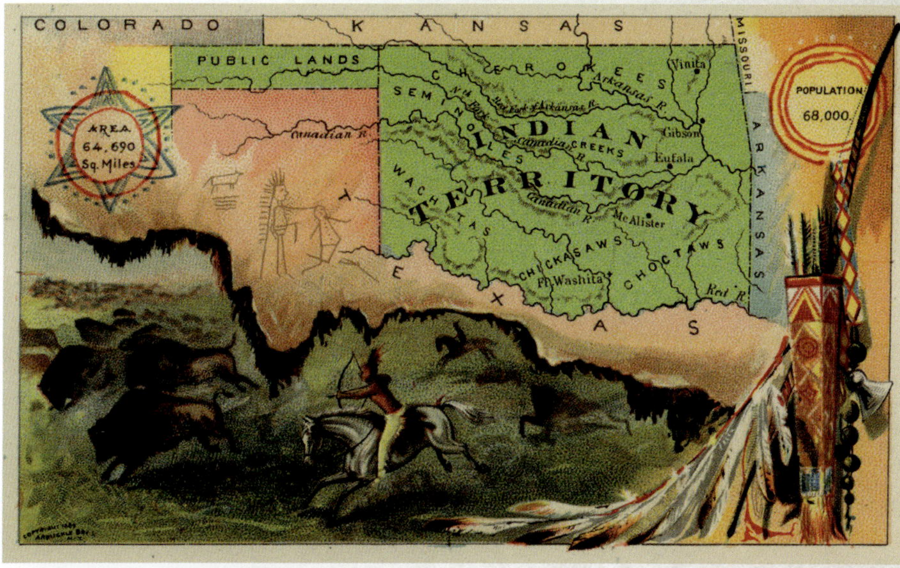


**Seen here is an 1889 map of Indian Territory from *Arbuckles' Illustrated Atlas of the United States of America*.**

It was believed this land was difficult for farming and that no white man would ever want to live there. After the Indian Removal Act was signed into law on May 28, 1830, President Andrew Jackson had the power to exchange land west of the Mississippi for the southeastern territory of the "Five Civilized Tribes"—the Cherokee, Creek, Choctaw, Chickasaw, and Seminole. The long, difficult journey of these peoples to their assigned homeland in the area called Indian Territory (now Oklahoma) in the middle of winter is known as the Trail of Tears. However, white settlers soon moved there, too.

In the late 1800s, the U.S. Army fought many battles against the native people of the Great Plains and the Southwest. One of the most famous was the Battle of the Little Bighorn in 1876. Many Plains Indians had rejected an order to retreat from land in the Dakota Territory west of the Missouri River after white gold miners settled there in defiance of a treaty. In the ensuing battle, Lieut. Col. George A. Custer and all of his men were killed. One of the last conflicts took place in 1890 at the village of Wounded Knee in South Dakota; in it, the U.S. Army massacred several hundred Native Americans. The episode, sometimes called the Battle of Wounded Knee, completed the conquest of the North American Indians.

Eventually, most of the Native Americans of the West came to live on reservations. Reservations are areas of land that the U.S. government set aside for certain Native American groups. However, a nation's reservation was often smaller or in a different place than its original homeland. Conditions on the reservations were poor.

## WILMA MANKILLER: FIRST WOMAN TO LEAD A MAJOR NATION

Born in Tahlequah, Oklahoma, Wilma Mankiller (1945–2010) was the sixth of eleven children born to a Cherokee father and a Dutch-Irish mother. She spent her early life on land given to her grandfather by the federal government after the Cherokee were forced to move to Oklahoma in the 1830s. In 1956 the family relocated again to California, a move she called "my own little Trail of Tears." In the mid-1970s, Mankiller moved back to Oklahoma. Activist groups sparked her interest in local government. In 1985, she became chief of the Cherokee, making her the first woman chief of a major Native American nation. She served in this role until 1995. Mankiller helped reform the nation's government and improve its people's education, health, and housing.

Wilma Mankiller is shown here at the 2005 American Indian College Fund Gala.

## Changes in Treatment

Beginning in the mid-1800s, the U.S. government followed a policy called assimilation. It attempted to force Native Americans to adopt the European way of life and moved them away from their ancestral homes to accommodate white settlers. The policy was largely unsuccessful. In 1926, a survey found most native peoples were "extremely poor," in bad health, without education, and isolated from white culture around them.

In 1934, the U.S. government began to change the way it treated Native Americans. It passed a law that gave Native American nations more power over their own affairs. The Indian Reorganization Act of 1934 reestablished the native nations as political groups—separate from the U.S. government—and promoted Native American culture and religion.

Many nations set up governments similar to that of the United States, with constitutions and laws, various branches of leadership (such as judicial, executive, and legislative branches), and elections by secret ballot. The new law also gave them money for buying back land that had been swindled from them, as well as money for educational and medical facilities.

However, by the 1950s, there were still many issues between Native Americans and the U.S. government. Things were not much better in Canada. In 1969, the Canadian government tried to end a protective law called the Indian Act. Native groups protested the government's actions. It sparked a surge in political activism among Canada's native people. New organizations advocated for native rights, improved education, and economic development.

In the United States, activists from a protest group called the American Indian Movement (AIM) occupied Alcatraz Island in San Francisco Bay for nineteen months in 1969–1971, claiming it as native land. In 1973, about two hundred armed AIM supporters occupied the village of Wounded Knee, the

**Glenn Morris of the American Indian Movement (AIM) speaks at a protest against a Columbus Day parade.**

## THE FORMATION OF AIM

The American Indian Movement (AIM) is one of many groups that fight for the rights of Native Americans. It was founded in 1968 by Native Americans in Minneapolis, Minnesota, who were seeking to help with issues including poverty, housing, and negative relationships with the police and government. Soon chapters of AIM began opening around the United States and Canada. AIM's work in the 1960s and 1970s drew national attention and inspired activists who continue to work for the cause today.

site of the 1890 battle of the same name, on the Oglala Sioux Pine Ridge Reservation in South Dakota in a seventy-one-day standoff.

The message was clear: native groups were frustrated and seeking rights. They wanted to have lands that were once theirs returned to them, and they pursued legal action to provide for the rights of their people.

## CHAPTER FIVE

# NATIVE NORTH AMERICANS TODAY

Native Americans, Alaska Natives, First Nations, Inuit, and Métis people have been among the world's most active and successful groups in bringing about political change. Since the late twentieth century they have made gains in areas such as education, land ownership, religious freedom, and law. They have worked to revitalize traditional culture by encouraging the use of native languages. They have also had some success in finding new sources of income to improve their economic standing.

## Modern Native Peoples

The U.S. government officially recognizes more than 560 nations, all eligible for government services. The largest include the Cherokee, Navajo, Sioux, and

Members of several Canadian First Nations, including the Dakota Sioux, the Dene, and the Cree, wear traditional clothing.

Ojibwa. The states with the largest native populations are California, Oklahoma, Arizona, Texas, and New Mexico. The 2010 census notes 5.2 million Native Americans and Alaska Natives live in the United States. They make up about 1.7 percent of the U.S. population.

In Canada, the number of people reporting First Nations, Métis, or Inuit ancestry reached one million in the early twenty-first century. The Cree are the largest of the more than six hundred nations recognized by the Canadian government. Native Canadian populations are highest in Ontario, British Columbia, Alberta, Manitoba, and Saskatchewan.

By the start of the twenty-first century, only about one-third of the native peoples in the United States lived on reservations and in other rural areas; the other two-thirds lived in cities or towns. In Canada, the number of native people living in urban areas reached 50 percent in the late twentieth century and continued to climb. These changes have had lasting effects on the economic, social, and cultural lives of both native individuals and their nations.

## Life on Reservations

In the United States, Indian reservations are concentrated in the West and in the Great Lakes region. The largest is the Navajo reservation, which covers about 16 million acres (6.5 million hectares) in Arizona, New Mexico, and Utah. Other large reservations include the Tohono O'odham reservation in Arizona, the Uintah and Ouray reservation in Utah, the Wind River reservation in Wyoming, the Fort Peck and Crow reservations in Montana, and three Sioux reservations—Pine Ridge, Cheyenne River, and Standing Rock—in the Dakotas.

# NATIVE AMERICANS IN YOUNG ADULT LITERATURE

In young adult fiction, Native Americans are often misrepresented as "mystical" people or characters from times long ago. Many books don't reflect the experience of modern native kids. Native American authors such as Sherman Alexie (of the Spokane and Coeur d'Alene), who wrote the 2007 National Book Award winner *The Absolutely True Diary of a Part-Time Indian*, are working to fight stereotypes by writing about the real experiences of Native Americans. Alexie believes that with young adult fiction "you can make real significant social change."

**Sherman Alexie (*third from left*) poses with other winners at the National Book Awards in 2007.**

Most U.S. and Canadian reservations were established in the nineteenth and early twentieth centuries. Usually they were placed on land that was difficult to develop. With limited economic opportunities, people often have to leave the reservation for higher education or employment. When compared with neighboring areas, reservations have historically tended to be underdeveloped in terms of roads, bridges, utilities, communication equipment, housing, and social services.

Reservations are outside the reach of state laws. This has allowed many nations to open casinos on their land. These businesses raise money and provide jobs.

On some reservations, slow local development has created high rates of poverty, substance abuse, and violence. However, many national organizations and local activists are working to improve their communities. Those who have left reservations continue to support residents by providing them with money and other forms of assistance. Casinos and cultural festivals also draw visitors.

**A woman sits with her children on the Navajo Indian reservation in Arizona.**

## Respect and Reparations

Native peoples continue to fight for the land they lost, reparations for past damages, and the respect of their history and culture. Native organizations continue to be active in political and social issues in both the United States and Canada. One such group in the United States is the National Congress of American Indians, which advocates for Indians and Alaska Natives. In Canada, major organizations include the Assembly of First Nations and the Congress of Aboriginal Peoples. Inuit interests are represented by the Inuit Circumpolar Council, formed in 1977 by the Inuit of Canada, Greenland, and Alaska.

**Members of Idle No More, a protest movement among Canada's First Nations, march in support of native rights in 2013.**

In 2014, the U.S. government agreed to pay $554 million to the Navajo Nation to settle a lawsuit brought by the tribe.

## SHOULD THE WASHINGTON REDSKINS CHANGE THEIR NAME?

A growing number of people want the Washington Redskins of the National Football League (NFL) to change their name. The team has had the name for more than eighty years. Its owner, Dan Snyder, argues that the name is a respectful salute to native people. Others say the term "redskin" is offensive. In May 2014, fifty U.S. senators wrote to NFL commissioner Roger Goodell to request a change. In June 2014, the U.S. Patent Office canceled the team's trademark, making it impossible for the team to sell products with the Redskins name. The team intends to appeal the ruling.

The suit claimed that the tribe's funds and resources had been mismanaged by the U.S. government for more than fifty years. Navajo Nation president Ben Shelly called it a "victory for tribal sovereignty," and the tribe agreed not to seek further damages. In 2012, the U.S. government had agreed to pay $1 billion to forty-one Native American tribes in similar settlements.

# GLOSSARY

**ABORIGINAL** Being the first of its kind in a region.

**ADAPT** To change so as to fit a new or specific use or situation.

**ADOBE** Sun-baked clay.

**ALLIANCE** A union between persons, families, or parties, particularly for protection or assistance.

**ANCESTOR** One from whom an individual, group, or species is descended.

**ARCTIC** The North Pole or the region around it; the subarctic regions are those below or outside the Arctic Circle.

**BAND** Family group that lives and works together.

**BISON** Either of two types of large shaggy-maned mammals related to the ox, with a large head, short horns, and a large fleshy hump above the shoulders; buffalo.

**CULTURE** The beliefs, social practices, and characteristics of a racial, religious, or social group.

**DOMESTICATED** Adapted to living with human beings and/or to serving their purposes.

**EXTINCT** No longer existing.

**KINSHIP** The state of being related.

**MIGRATION** The act or an instance of migrating, or moving from one country, place, or locality to another.

**NATION (OR TRIBE)** A community of people that includes many families and relatives who share the same language, customs, and beliefs.

**PALEO-** Ancient or old; Paleo-Indians were the earliest people in North America.

**PEMMICAN** Dried lean meat pounded fine and mixed with melted fat.

**RESERVATION** An area of public land that is reserved, or set aside, for Native Americans.

**TEPEE** A cone-shaped tent usually of skins used as a home especially by Native Americans of the Great Plains.

**TUBER** Short, thick stem that is part of certain plants (such as the potato), that grows underground, and that can produce a new plant.

FOR MORE INFORMATION

Costain, Diane. *Native Americans of the Great Plains* (Discovery Education: Ancient Civilizations). New York, NY: PowerKids Press, 2013.

Gagne, Tammy. *Life on the Reservations* (State of Affairs: Native Americans in the 21st Century). Hockessin, DE: Mitchell Lane Publishers, 2014.

Kavin, Kim. *Native Americans: Discover the History and Cultures of the First Americans* (Build It Yourself). White River Junction, VT: Nomad Press, 2013.

Kuiper, Kathleen, ed. *Indigenous Peoples of the Arctic, Subarctic, and Northwest Coast* (Native American Tribes). New York, NY: Rosen Publishing, 2012.

Kuiper, Kathleen, ed. *Native American Culture* (Native American Sourcebook). New York, NY: Britannica/Rosen Publishing, 2011.

Mattern, Joanne. *Native Americans and the U.S. Government* (State of Affairs: Native Americans in the 21st Century). Hockessin, DE: Mitchell Lane Publishers, 2014.

Silvey, Diane. *The Kids Book of Aboriginal Peoples in Canada*. Toronto, ON: Kids Can Press, 2012.

Zimmerman, Larry J. *Exploring the Life, Myth, and Art of Native Americans* (Civilizations of the World). New York, NY: Rosen Publishing, 2010.

## Websites

Because of the changing nature of Internet links, Rosen Publishing has developed an online list of websites related to the subject of this book. This site is updated regularly. Please use this link to access this list:

http://www.rosenlinks.com/ANCIV/Amer

INDEX

## A



## B



## C



## E



## F



## G



## H



## I



## K



## L